AF342249

Photo by Jonathan Slaff

Daniel Martin, Christine Parks, Rebecca Harris, David Johnson and Cheryl Haas in the Theater for the New City production of "True Crimes." Set design by E. David Cosier and Romulus Linney.

TRUE CRIMES

BY ROMULUS LINNEY

★

DRAMATISTS
PLAY SERVICE
INC.

For my wife

Laura Patrice Callanan

TRUE CRIMES received its premiere at Theater for the New City (Crystal Field, Executive Director), in New York City, in December, 1995. It was directed by Romulus Linney; the assistant director was Heather Hill; the set design was by E. David Cosier and Romulus Linney; the costume design was by Jonathan Green; the lighting design was by Jeffrey S. Koger; the technical directors were Mark Mercante and David Scott and the stage manager was Anthony Pick. The cast was as follows:

LOGAN LOVEL .... David Johnson
JENNIE NOTREE .... Heather Melton
MARY SPARKS .... Cheryl Haas
VANGEY LOVEL .... Christine Parks
AB LOVEL .... Daniel Martin
SOONY SPARKS .... Fred Burrell
NANCY SPARKS.. Rebecca Harris
SAWDUST .... Mark Alan Gordon
A VOICE IN THE WIND .... Erin Hill

CHARACTERS

LOGAN LOVEL
JENNIE NOTREE, his mistress
MARY SPARKS, his mistress
VANGEY LOVEL, his mother
AB LOVEL, his father
SOONY SPARKS, Mary Sparks's husband
NANCY SPARKS, Soony Sparks's daughter from his first
       marriage
SAWDUST, a migrant farmhand
A VOICE IN THE WIND

PLACE

The Appalachian Mountains

TIME

1900

TRUE CRIMES is taken from pamphlets and newspapers of 19th-century America and from an event in Tula, Russia, as used by Leo Tolstoy in his play, THE POWER OF DARKNESS.

It is played without intermission.

TRUE CRIMES

Cheerful Appalachian music.

A wooden platform, the porch of a substantial mountain house. Around it lie a front yard and two nearby places, one marked by a piece of a split-rail fence, the other by a tree stump or a large rock.

On the platform is a rocking chair, with a colorful quilt over it. Two old slat chairs, a crate, and a chest holding whiskey and glasses are the only other furnishings.

Behind the platform is a wall of Appalachian mountain strip quilts. The quilts are those made by poor people not for art but for warmth, from flour sacks and strips of colorful cloth. This wall of quilts represents the house of Soony Sparks, through which characters can enter and exit.*

At center, on the stage floor, is another, very shabby quilt.

Music ends. Lights up on the shabby quilt. Logan is telling Jennie, very enthusiastically, what's in a penny dreadful "True Crime" pamphlet he holds in his hands.

LOGAN.   A woman gets raped. A tramp gets arrested. A judge tells the jury if they find the tramp guilty they have to hang that tramp and they do. Year later, it turns out the tramp was innocent and the judge's own son raped that woman. These stories always end with a poem. Here's this one. *(He recites the first part of the poem, reads the rest.)*

* See Special Note on copyright page.

"Old Judge Beal, he spared himself his life.
But with a shiny knife,
He sawed from its root his eloquent tongue.
Then he put it in a pan
And fried it like a man,
And ate it on the spot that tramp was hung."
JENNIE.   Oh, Logan.
LOGAN.   What?
JENNIE.   People getting raped. Cutting off their tongues and eating them. My Lord.
LOGAN.   I didn't make up the world, that's the way it is!
JENNIE.   Oh, Logan.
LOGAN.   Wimmen have babies, men learn. That's why I read these books! I got a mind! I could be a lawyer, or a judge myself! I could be a detective at least, or a sheriff or something! I have dreams!
JENNIE.   But not about me. *(No answer.)* You got no use for me today, do you? *(No answer.)* Thought you wanted me, you read me a murder story instead.
LOGAN.   Hoped you'd like it.
JENNIE.   You're leaving me.
LOGAN.   We knowed we would come to this.
JENNIE.   *You* might have! I never did!
LOGAN.   I can't marry no woman about to marry some other man!
JENNIE.   I don't want to marry no other man!
LOGAN.   Anson Tate tells the world he's asked you twict!
JENNIE.   Three times! And he's fifty-eight-year old!! But what do you want me to do? Tell him, fly away? He will!! God knows I'd never have him if you'll have me!
LOGAN.   Well, I won't! *(Pause.)*
JENNIE.   Mary Sparks has a husband, too.
LOGAN.   Watch out, now!
JENNIE.   Mary Sparks is just as married as I'll be, Logan.
LOGAN.   I said watch out!
JENNIE.   LOGAN!
LOGAN.   WHAT?
JENNIE.   Just say it! Never no more!

LOGAN.   NEVER NO MORE!

JENNIE.   I should a known! But Mary Sparks? That woman's no good, Logan!

LOGAN.   Shut your mouth about her!

JENNIE.   She married an old man for his money!

LOGAN.   Like you will Anson Tate!

JENNIE.   But I don't *want* Anson Tate! I want you!

LOGAN.   Enough of this. Goodbye!!

JENNIE.   No! Just won't see you, that's all. We were children together, and that will never change. And that is something. It's a *sort* of happiness. Just take care what married woman you play with, hear? Husbands have shotguns.

LOGAN.   I can take care of myself!

JENNIE.   Spect so! If you find a better one, you'll forget me. But if a worse one, you'll remember. Bye.

LOGAN.   Bye. *(Exit Jennie. Sprightly music. Change of light. Enter Mary Sparks. She sits on Logan's quilt, watching him. Lights come up as Logan enthusiastically describes another "True Crime.")* Five-hundred-dollar reward out for Fatty Harper, but Fatty Harper weighs four hundred pound. Sidney Creed, on a sick mule, tracks Fatty Harper to a camp by a river fifty mile into the wilderness. Pulls his gun! But how you going to tote a four hundred pound man fifty mile anywhere on a sick mule? There's blue clay in that river bed. Sidney Creed shoots Fatty Harper in the back, saws off his head, and packs it in blue clay! Now's here's the poem! *(Reciting.)*

> "Scandal!" says the town.
> "Awful!" says the crowd.
> "Illegal!" says the Sheriff.
> Says the Law, "It's allowed.""

(Reading.)

> Inside the ball of blue that day,
> Was a head you couldn't call handsome,
> But when that clay got scraped away,
> The Judge said, "Here's the ransom!""

MARY.   Logan! *(Mary, who has been staring at Logan with plain lust, jumps on him. They grind passionately, then hastily begin to undo buttons on each other's clothes. Enter Vangey Lovel and Ab*

Lovel. Vangey wears strong thick mountain clothes. Ab wears a black suit, worn but impressive. They stroll up to the writhing couple on the quilt and stand by, smiling.)
VANGEY.   Hidy-do.
AB.   Son.
MARY.   Oh, my God! *(Logan scrambles away. Mary jumps up, turns away buttoning up her dress.)*
VANGEY.   Mary Sparks, ain't it? Reckon you know my husband, Ab.
AB.   Thought we'd say hidy.
VANGEY.   You don't have to button up no dress for me.
AB.   It's human nature.
VANGEY.   How's your husband? *(Mary turns back around.)*
MARY.   Just fine.
AB.   Ain't what we hear.
VANGEY.   Sick, sick man.
MARY.   He is at times.
AB.   How, exactly?
VANGEY.   Have a seat. You are concerned about our boy. We are concerned about you. *(Mary sits back on the quilt.)*
MARY.   Six weeks coughing blood.
VANGEY.   What's it look like?
MARY.   Bright red.
VANGEY.   Does it ever look like there's dirt in it?
MARY.   Sort of. *(Vangey sits on the quilt next to Mary.)*
VANGEY.   Does that dirt ever look sort of like red coffee grounds?
MARY.   Sometimes.
VANGEY.   Can he work?
MARY.   He works me instead. And his daughter. We tend him day and night. *(Ab sits on the quilt next to Vangey. They are all four sitting there now, in a sort of conference.)*
AB.   You have a man living there. He prays with me. Calls hisself Sawdust.
MARY.   He lives in the barn.
AB.   A drunkard. Reformed, thanks to God.
MARY.   Sawdust told you about me?
AB.   And our boy.

VANGEY.   And your husband sick.
AB.   It is a predicament.
VANGEY.   Farm? What happens to it?
MARY.   Bob Stoneman's dogs herd for us. Carson twins owe my husband money so they plow some and harrow. Sawdust the rest.
AB.   Two hundred acre?
MARY.   Two hundred and five.
AB.   Hard work!
MARY.   Not another word! What's this for?
VANGEY.   I grub plants and roots, while our boy has to clerk at a dry goods store. That's what this is about.
AB.   We could all do better.
VANGEY.   Let me say it this way. I want more pleasure out of my life than I get right now. How about you?
MARY.   There are things I want.
AB.   God made us like that.
VANGEY.   I know everthing living in these mountains. Herbs and roots and plants and whatever grows, I pick it all. But I'm sick of bending over for it.
AB.   Life is hard.
VANGEY.   You fancy our son.
MARY.   Won't deny that.
VANGEY.   He's a lady killer. You deny that?
MARY.   No.
VANGEY.   Not no genius but strong and juicy.
AB.   A tree that might bear fruit.
VANGEY.   Wimmen flock around him like crows over corn. But I'll talk turkey, if you'll talk squirrel. Got to have him?
MARY.   Come on, now! Turkey and squirrel!
LOGAN.   What are you talking about?
VANGEY.   Her husband's sick. He's fixing to die. That's what we're talking about. *(Pause.)* Are we?
MARY.   We could be.
AB.   Can't plow?
MARY.   No.
AB.   Sawdust the only working man there?
MARY.   Yes.

VANGEY.   You need another man around the place.
MARY.   Oh.
VANGEY.   We'll come by Sunday, if you'll have us. *(Vangey and Ab get up.)* To discuss it properly with your husband. Come on with us, Logan. *(Logan and Mary get up. Vangey and Logan fold up Logan's old quilt.)*
AB.   Some decent hour after church. I am preaching miracles. Loaves and fishes, and the water into wine! Come on, son!
MARY.   Early afternoon?
VANGEY.   We'll be there.
LOGAN.   Now just a minute.
VANGEY.   Hush. Possess your soul in patience, Logan.
AB.   God is good. *(Sprightly music. Exit Vangey, Ab and Logan. Light fades on Mary looking after them. Exit Mary. Light up on the porch. Enter Soony Sparks, through the wall of quilts, a man in his 60s, ill. He sits in his rocking chair, wraps himself in the colorful quilt. He opens a chest next to his chair, takes out a bottle of whiskey and a glass, pours half a drink, settles down. Enter Mary, with a bowl of spoon bread.)*
MARY.   Eat the spoonbread, Soony, afore the likker.
SOONY.   Whiskey first.
MARY.   If you eat right, you'll outlive every soul in these mountains.
SOONY.   Maybe.
MARY.   No maybe about it. Come on, now, chew down what I fixed you.
SOONY.   I'll try! *(Enter Vangey, Ab and Logan, carrying his book. They stand in front of the porch.)*
VANGEY.   *(Calling.)* Hidy!
MARY.   Well, hey there, Miz Lovel. Mister Lovel. Logan.
AB.   Hidy, Misses. Hidy, Soony.
SOONY.   Who's that?
MARY.   The Lovels, Soony. Vangey, Ab and Logan.
SOONY.   What do Lovels want here? *(Enter Nancy Sparks, Soony's young daughter by an earlier marriage. She wears boy's overalls and looks very childish. With her is Sawdust, a weather-beaten, very agreeable migrant farm hand.)*
MARY.   Be pleasant, and we'll see. *(To Lovels.)* Come up on

the porch.

VANGEY. Pleased to. *(The Lovels go onto the porch. Nancy comes up on the porch. Vangey looks around.)* Just as pretty a home as the flowers are made. Can you see all your land from your porch here?

MARY. Pert near. Yonder's the state line, down by them tulip trees. My husband Soony built this porch hisself, thirty year ago.

VANGEY. It's a fine residence on a solid subsistence. *(To Nancy.)* Hidy.

NANCY. *(To Vangey.)* Hidy.

VANGEY. What you got there?

MARY. What you got there, Nancy?

NANCY. Sawdust made me a whimmey-diddle. See? *(Nancy works a crude mountain toy, with a man on one end of a see-saw and a bear on the other. She works it for Mary and Vangey.)*

SAWDUST. There he is! *(Sawdust pushes Nancy towards Ab. She works the toy in front of him.)* The Bear and the Preacher! *(Sawdust points at Ab, and all laugh.)*

AB. That's me, all right! *(They all settle on the porch.)*

MARY. Good of you, Sawdust. *(To Lovels.)* When Nancy's Mamma died and I married Soony here, I said Nancy'd be looked after, and she is. Her and Sawdust are what you call chums.

SOONY. Chums is two boys, woman, don't you know nothing at all?

MARY. Looked after is the point, Soony. Your daughter is.

SOONY. Ain't denying that.

MARY. Now, then, let's have some refreshment on a Sunday afternoon. Nancy.

NANCY. Yes, ma'am. *(Mary and Nancy open the old chest and produce cups and whiskey.)*

AB. Sawdust?

SAWDUST. Not a drop for me. You know that.

AB. I plain admire the man who gives up whiskey for the Lord.

SAWDUST. You helped me do it.

AB. We prayed together, is all. Any news of your wife?

SAWDUST.   No.

AB.   Maybe there will be. She'll get saved somewhere, and come back to you.

SAWDUST.   I pray for it.

AB.   So do we. *(Nancy passes around a tray of mugs and mason jar glasses. Mary pours Soony's whiskey in them for everyone.)*

MARY.   So. How was church?

VANGEY.   Pleasant as worship can be.

MARY.   Sawdust says you preach powerful salvation. What's the name of your church?

AB.   Free Word of Life Amalgamated Trinity. My congregations come and go, as they please. You give me a church in a building in one place and I'll give you the devil. I preach to them what purely follows God. You see, God is what's important. Churches say this, do that, like this, like that, but that ain't God.

MARY.   What is?

AB.   Something entirely otherwise! *(Nancy passes out whiskey to everyone.)*

VANGEY.   My husband, Mr. Sparks, would have made a wonderful Baptist or Methodist or Presbyterian preacher if he'd a ever gone to school, but he never did. He tried, but he couldn't.

MARY.   He must know the Bible pretty well.

VANGEY.   He has a memory powerful particular.

MARY.   Sawdust, don't you want some spring water, or something?

SAWDUST.   Not one drop of nothing.

MARY.   Nancy?

NANCY.   Can I?

SOONY.   Give the child a dollop. Let her learn. *(He gives her some of his whiskey.)*

MARY.   So here's to us. Neighbors, all.

ALL.   *(Drinking.) Here's to that! Yes, sir! Yes, ma'm! (They all drink, but with care at first, not knowing what Soony's corn whiskey will be like. It is harsh and they feel it burn but not bad, in fact, good.) Ahh! Yes, ma'am. Yes, sir. (They drink in sips then gulps. A contented pause.)*

MARY.   Well, the dogwoods are out.

VANGEY.   Gums, too.

MARY.   Bright red berries in the dogwood.

VANGEY.   And leaves in the gum trees red as fire. With your sourwoods on the peak of color, I swear they are.

MARY.   Your goldenrod and asters, don't forget them.

VANGEY.   Never in this world. Now, just roadside everwhere, your birch and tulip poplar are gold, sassafras is flame, sumac a sort of carmine, and the sugar maple, well, them sassy things is a-blazing just everwhere.

SOONY.   Damn wimmen. We going to sit here and talk about trees all day? *(They all keep drinking. Mary and Vangey keep the conversation going.)*

MARY.   I hear Mrs. Morse over at Turner's Cove had a hard baby.

VANGEY.   At's a fact I can attest to. I was the midwife. Well, me and Sarah Starns. Lord God, it was touch and it was go. At baby weighted eleven maybe twelve pound, and was aiming to come out kicking feet first. Sarah, she pressed it and moved it a tad and I tried, too, but we was feared of the worst. It was a certain killing of Tillie Morse dead in bed. We got the lights low, her fool husband quiet, and we worked and we worked. Now, I tell you this. Five minute afore that thing was born, it commenced, commenced to turn — near as I can say it, like a crow or a raven sailing in the air over a mountain updraft. Or it was like some big old fat trout in a river, down at the bottom and staying there. But when it come, Sarah Starns breathing like a bellows, it just slipped out, flop, like that! I mean, hit was a baby and not no bird or no fish! There was a river, but it was blood! At big fat thing, mad and screaming rage, come out at us like a bull out of a barn. Shoo!

SOONY.   Get these people the hell out of here.

MARY.   Soony, hush.

SOONY.   Well, something else besides flowers and bloody babies! *(Ab suddenly stands up.)*

AB.   Testify to us, Sawdust! I'll get right down with you! *(Ab kneels.)* This man had a home! Likker took it! *(Sawdust comes on the porch, and kneels before them, hands held up in the air. The others quietly drink.)*

SAWDUST.   Onct upon a time a fool had a wife! They were younguns right healthy, rejoicing in the strength of their ways! But it didn't last, since nothing that is flesh ever does!

AB.   Amen!

SAWDUST.   They drank together, then alone, then with whoever wherever. The fool I speak of last seen that wife on a roadhouse floor, on her knees between some scoundrel's legs, begging for whatever was left in his glass. The fool was me and I ran! I prayed to God with Ab Lovel's help, sweated my insides out, quit drinking and found this job here! Amen! *(Sawdust gets up, sits on the porch again. Ab goes back to his chair.)*

AB.   Amen!

SAWDUST.   And I'm thankful to Ab Lovel! He showed me what whiskey, and prayer to fight it, can do.

AB.   Glory to God, and respects to you. *(Ab takes up his whiskey.)* And in temperate moderation, thanks for this.

MARY.   What happened in your church today?

AB.   Sang a good old hymn.

VANGEY.   My husband is eternally preoccupied with hymns.

SOONY.   I ain't got nothing against hymns.

MARY.   Sing it for us.

AB.   "His Life On Earth!" *(Singing.)*

    AND DIDST THOU LOVE THE RACE
    THAT LOVED NOT THEE,
    AND DIDST THOU TAKE TO HEAV'N
    A HUMAN BROW?
    DOEST PLEAD WITH MAN'S VOICE
    BY THE MARVELOUS SEA?
    ART THOU HIS KINSMAN NOW?

(Ab drinks.)

SOONY.   At's powerful spiny. Sing it through. Can't do me no harm. *(Ab stands up, a commanding presence.)*

AB.   *(Singing.)*

    BY THAT ONE LIKENESS
    WHICH IS OURS AND THINE,
    BY THAT ONE NATURE*

* See Special Note on Songs and Recordings on copyright page.

WHICH DOTH HOLD US KIN,
   BY THAT HIGH HEAVEN WHERE
   SINLESS THOU DOTH SHINE,
   TO DRAW US SINNERS IN;

Glory.
NANCY.   It is strong.
SOONY.   I'm feeling better. Where's that whiskey?
MARY.   Right here.
NANCY.   Bet I can hum it now.
AB.   Then do, child! Glory to God! *(Ab sings to Nancy who sings it back at him. The rest join in. Mary pours out whiskey, ending up with Logan. Everyone but Sawdust is drinking a lot of whiskey. Singing, with Nancy joining in.)*

   FOR THY LAST SILENCE
   IN THE JUDGMENT HALL,
   BY LONG FOREKNOWLEDGE
   OF THE DEADLY TREE,
   BY DARKNESS, BY THE WORMWOOD
   AND THE GALL,
   I PRAY THOU VISIT ME.

Nancy! Praise God!
SOONY.   Peculiar, at hymn, but I like it!
MARY.   Good, Soony! Drink up, honey.
SOONY.   I will! Sing that again!
AB.   *(Ab goes by each one, singing, with others joining in.)*
   BY THY LAST SILENCE
   IN THE JUDGMENT HALL,
   BY LONG FOREKNOWLEDGE
   OF THE DEADLY TREE,
   BY DARKNESS, BY THE WORMWOOD
   AND THE GALL,
   I PRAY THOU VISIT ME.*

Oh, wretched sinner. Oh forgotten Lord. Oh, this hard, hard life. Freedom from sin, where is it? You know it's in the Power! Let the Power *move* on you. Let it *freeze* that sin, let it *burn* that sin, let it *sing* that sin away. What will you say, oh sinner,

* See Special Note on Songs and Recordings on copyright page.

when you stand naked before the Lamb, the naked Lamb, holding his scepter in his — paws — with the crown of heaven on his head, a naked Lamb sitting on a golden throne by the ever flowing river of God! HIS LIFE ON EARTH, bring at last verse home again!

SOONY.   Sing to the Lord! What the hell!!!! *(They stand up, ramrod straight, shouting and singing. They are very rigid and very drunk, except for Sawdust and Vangey, who sing loudly with them.)*

ALL.

> BY THY LAST SILENCE
> IN THE JUDGMENT HALL,
> BY LONG FOREKNOWLEDGE
> OF THE DEADLY TREE
> BY DARKNESS, BY THE WORMWOOD
> AND THE GALL,
> I PRAY THOU VISIT ME.*

(Soony has a sudden, terrible coughing fit. He knocks over his chair and almost falls. Mary, Nancy and Ab grab him, settle him back in his chair, comforted by his quilt. They all watch him closely.)

SOONY.   Enjoyed the hymn.

AB.   Hallelujah.

SOONY.   Hallelujah.

VANGEY.   Let me say this before my husband sings us to death. What we want to do is be of help to you.

SOONY.   Can them herbs of yours, them logan-bark spells and split-gizzard poultices, give a body a new lungs and kidney?

VANGEY.   Reckon not.

SOONY.   What can?

VANGEY.   I don't know. But herb doctoring might help. Tolerate this in your whiskey.

SOONY.   What is it?

VANGEY.   Just cherry bark bitters, ground up in some freshness. Here. *(She holds out a folded kerchief, folded paper in it, opens it, and tastes from her little finger the powders held in it.)* Make ye tingle.

* See Special Note on Songs and Recordings on copyright page.

SOONY.   In the whiskey?

VANGEY.   That's where it's best.

SOONY.   All right. *(Vangey puts some in Soony's whiskey.)* And look here, Soony, I got something else can help you out, too.

MARY.   *(Quickly.)* What is that, Vangey?

VANGEY.   Our boy Logan. He's plain exasperated, working in town at the hardware store. We know you got Sawdust employed, a fine sober handyman, but this is a sizable estate. It needs intelligent management and more than two hands. *(Referring to whiskey and herbs.)* How is that?

SOONY.   Just fine.

VANGEY.   Just sip on it, Soony. You getting everything done you ought to?

SOONY.   God, no.

VANGEY.   Logan. *(Logan stands up quickly.)*

LOGAN.   I could come work for you.

SOONY.   For what? Can't pay no salary.

LOGAN.   Wouldn't need none.

SOONY.   He ain't working for nothing!

VANGEY.   Let our son farm that gulch land around Foster's creek. You don't use it. Let us cash rent it, with Logan working your farm as the cash rent. That's all I have to say.

SOONY.   This might not be unheard of.

MARY.   Handsome offer, Soony.

VANGEY.   Logan's smart. Reads books. Tell Soony what you think about his milking, Logan. *(Logan goes to Soony.)*

LOGAN.   Five people died milk sick in this county, this year. I can protect your cows, and you and your wife.

SOONY.   No, you can't. Nobody knows how to keep a cow from giving sick milk.

LOGAN.   There's this here little book about it. *(Logan pulls a government pamphlet from the pages of his "True Crime" book.)* See? Says Farm Bureau, United States Government. "Milk Sickness and How To Stop It."

SOONY.   What does that other'n say?

LOGAN.   "True Crime" book. *(Logan moves away, leaving Soony the pamphlet.)* I get them both in the mail.

VANGEY.   So what do you say, Soony?

SOONY.   His room and board?
VANGEY.   You got to do *something* for him!
MARY.   He can sleep in the barn loft. Make it up like a little house for you, Logan.
LOGAN.   That'd be good.
MARY.   I'd cook for him, too. There's enough.
VANGEY.   Soony?
SOONY.   Nancy?
NANCY.   He's a nice man, Daddy.
LOGAN.   I'll make you some whimmey-diddles you ain't seen yet.
NANCY.   I'll hold you to it!
AB.   So, Soony, for Christ's sweet sake hanging bloody off the cross, what do you say?
SOONY.   I say yes. Logan, welcome to our home.
MARY.   Here's to you, Logan!
VANGEY.   Let's drink to it!
MARY.   To Logan!
ALL.   To Logan!! *(They laugh and drink. Brisk music. Exeunt all but Logan. Music. Change of light. Time passes. Logan looks around, pleased with himself and what he sees. Enter Sawdust, working on a lock. Logan sits on the edge of the porch reading his "True Crime" book to Sawdust, who stands by.)*
LOGAN.   Lumberjack Jake chops a harlot with an axe. Then he cuts her in two, a bosom on each side. What does his lawyer say? "My client done it in his sleep, and is therefore a son-a-bu-list and is therefore innocent." The jury considered that carefully, before they hung him.
SAWDUST.   That right?
LOGAN.   Here's the poem wrote about it.

    " "I was asleep," said Lumberjack Jake,
      "Dreaming of beautiful trees."
      But he was awake
      And he was a fake
      "With an axe and a beautiful tease."
      When she asked him for money,
      He said, "Right now, honey,"
      And he split her clean down to her knees."

(*Logan stares at Sawdust.*) What do you think about that?
SAWDUST.   At there is violence. I don't care for it.
LOGAN.   It's life, ain't it?
SAWDUST.   Don't have to be.
LOGAN.   But it is, all the time.
SAWDUST.   For some, but not for others.
LOGAN.   How about for you?
SAWDUST.   I aim to get by without it. I've had enough trouble with my wife, thank you, to go rummage around wanting any vice or crime. I mean I thought the world was more better than it is, yessir. Like everybody else, I got taught otherwise. That there is life.
LOGAN.   Well, what else is life, Sawdust?
SAWDUST.   Just one damned thing after another, far a man like me. But you have to face it like an honest soul, with the help of a good preacher and god-fearing wimmen. I'm trying to find one and learn that.
LOGAN.   Yeah, well. When you going to work on the barn wall like I asked you?
SAWDUST.   Got to cook me some glue first.
LOGAN.   So get to it. (*Exit Sawdust. Logan stretches, looks about and exits, repeating and memorizing the poem. To himself.*)
      "I was asleep," the lumberjack said, "dreaming of
           beautiful trees."
(*Music.*)
      "He was awake," the sheriff said, "with an axe and a
           beautiful tease."
(*Exit Logan. Enter Mary. Paces, waiting. Enter Vangey. Mary runs to her.*)
VANGEY.   So what is it?
MARY.   Trouble.
VANGEY.   All right. Where's Logan?
MARY.   He's in the barn, asleep!
VANGEY.   Hold on! (*Out of the house steps Soony, with Nancy. He is talking to her. Vangey and Mary move to one side.*) First off, what's the matter?
MARY.   Soony knows.
VANGEY.   I figured he might.

MARY.   We never done it in the house.
VANGEY.   Nancy.
MARY.   I reckon. She fancies Logan, too.
VANGEY.   Ain't surprised.
MARY.   She ain't so innocent as she pretends.
VANGEY.   She jealous?
MARY.   Yes. Now what?
VANGEY.   Sooner than later, is all. I have what's needed.
(They turn to the porch.)
SOONY.   *(To Nancy.)* Get her here to me.
NANCY.   *(To Soony.)* Yes, Poppa. *(Soony goes back into the house. Nancy steps off the porch. Mary stops her.)*
MARY.   Where you going, Nancy?
NANCY.   Down the road.
MARY.   Where to, honey?
NANCY.   Ain't supposed to say.
MARY.   You can talk to me.
NANCY.   No, I can't.
VANGEY.   Well, me, then. I'm just this old woman.
MARY.   Listen to her, Nancy. She's our friend. *(Vangey moves between them, whispering to Mary.)*
VANGEY.   Go get Logan! *(Exit Mary. Vangey has a woman-to woman talk with Nancy, sitting down on the edge of the porch.)* You seen Logan and your stepmomma kissing, that it?
NANCY.   Might be.
VANGEY.   And him feeling her all over?
NANCY.   Might be.
VANGEY.   And her doing the same to him?
NANCY.   Yes, ma'am.
VANGEY.   I reckon your daddy didn't feel too good about it, when you told him. But how about you? How did you feel about it?
NANCY.   Funny.
VANGEY.   Wouldn't you like to be doing that?
NANCY.   Someday.
VANGEY.   Plain natural. Your daddy's sick and your step-momma's still young.
NANCY.   Reckon.

VANGEY.   Fine boy like Logan. You'd fancy that, now tell the truth.
NANCY.   Be content with it.
VANGEY.   So, leave your stepmomma and Logan be. They ain't hurting nobody. But I mean for you to do what your daddy told you. Which was what?
NANCY.   Bring him his sister.
VANGEY.   Martha Stiles?
NANCY.   Yes, ma'am. *(Vangey gets up.)*
VANGEY.   Well, let's do that! If you'll wait at the fence, I'll go see Martha Stiles with you. We'll stop on the way by Crawford Store and see what's on the counter. You fancy that?
NANCY.   Yes, ma'am.
VANGEY.   Good, honey. Here's a piece of ginger root. You chew on that and wait for me. I'll be right back. *(Vangey sits Nancy on the rock, who chews the ginger root. Enter Mary. Vangey goes to her.)* He's sending for his sister.
MARY.   Oh, God.
VANGEY.   Where does he keep it?
MARY.   His money? In a lock box.
VANGEY.   You've looked?
MARY.   He told me.
VANGEY.   What was in it?
MARY.   Farm titles and abstracts.
VANGEY.   Cash.
MARY.   Yes.
VANGEY.   How much cash?
MARY.   He said near six thousand dollar.
VANGEY.   God Amighty? In bills?
MARY.   Yes.
VANGEY.   Ain't it there now?
MARY.   He don't pay no attention to the box no more. *(Vangey turns toward the porch and walks to it.)*
VANGEY.   Then I reckon he's got it on him. *(Mary joins her.)*
MARY.   But I bathe him.
VANGEY.   He could hide it from you.
MARY.   He sends me out. Calls me back.
VANGEY.   When you sleep at night, is he nekkid?

MARY.   Never.

VANGEY.   Does he sleep on his stomach or one side?

MARY.   On his side, away from me.

VANGEY.   My Uncle Raymond did it that way. Everthing he owned on a string around his neck. That's where he's put it. Why do you reckon Soony sent for his sister?

MARY.   Why?

VANGEY.   To give it to her. You'll lose everthing. Husband, farm, Logan, everthing!

MARY.   That can't be!

VANGEY.   It don't have to. You love my son?

MARY.   Yes!

VANGEY.   Here. *(Vangey holds out the folded kerchief, and unfolds it, exposing a folded paper.)*

MARY.   What's this?

VANGEY.   Far as you know, it's cherry bark bitters, that's all.

MARY.   Oh, God, no!

VANGEY.   That man will leave this farm to his sister who will throw you out over the fence and she and that half wit daughter will own this place. That's one way things will be. The other is, let the man pass on not in his time but right now.

MARY.   Oh, God!

VANGEY.   Make up your mind.

MARY.   I never meant we'd kill him!

VANGEY.   Just wait?

MARY.   'Til he died by hisself!

VANGEY.   What I been doing here? I'll take my boy and go home!

MARY.   Don't do that!

VANGEY.   I said, make up your mind!!

MARY.   Won't it hurt him? Won't he yell and scream?

VANGEY.   He'll sleep first. Then he'll get cold, but wake up too late. All there is to it. *(Vangey holds out to Mary the folded papers in the folded kerchief.)* Make out like you're leaving. But stay, any way you can until he gets sick again. Then get it to him. But with *him* taking it! Don't *you* give it to him! *He* takes it!

MARY.   Oh, Lord! *(Mary takes the kerchief. Enter Logan.)*

LOGAN.   Hey! (*Vangey rushes to Logan.*)
VANGEY.   Just do what I tell you.
LOGAN.   Huh? (*Vangey slaps him, pushes him.*)
VANGEY.   WHAT I TELL YOU! (*Vangey goes to the steps on the porch.*) Soony! Soony! Come out on the porch, man, so's I can confess to you! (*Enter Soony, slowly. He stares at Vangey, then at Logan and Mary standing guilty together. He sits in his chair, pulls his quilt around him, glares at Vangey.*) Hidy, Soony.
SOONY.   Vangey Lovel, you done me wrong.
VANGEY.   I know it.
SOONY.   I trusted you Lovels. (*Vangey goes onto the porch.*)
VANGEY.   We trusted, too, in our boy and your wife! Both wrong! I stand here mortified with myself and my boy. And he is, too. Logan?
LOGAN.   Yes, ma'am.
VANGEY.   Say "I'm mortified at myself, Soony." (*Logan starts toward Soony.*)
LOGAN.   I'm mortified at —
SOONY.   I DON'T BELIEVE NONE OF YOU LOVELS!!!!
(*Logan scampers back.*)
VANGEY.   I wouldn't neither! Can't hold you to nothing we ever said. They fell to it. But remember your own hot blood, what a lusty man you was, in your day. Forgive my son. Forgive your wife. Make it up, and live in peace. Logan, you are a damned scoundrel. We will disgrace our friend's house no more. Come with me. (*Vangey and Logan step off the platform, leaving Sooney and Mary staring at each other. Vangey pushes Logan off. To Logan.*) Now git your daddy here! Drunk or sober, jest git him here! (*Exit Logan. Vangey goes by Mary, whispering to her.*) Talk to him. (*Vangey keeps going, to Nancy. Mary and Soony stare at each other. Mary slowly goes up on the porch. Vangey goes to Nancy, who has been waiting for her.*) Nancy, honey, here I am. Your daddy and your stepmomma are making it up. Let's give them a chance fore we go see your Aunt Martha. Come on with me. I'll show you some things you can pick in these woods you didn't know about. Make you a spell.
NANCY.   A charm for a man?
VANGEY.   If you want one. (*Exit Vangey and Nancy.*)

MARY.   I couldn't help it, Soony.
SOONY.   Fell to it, did ye?
MARY.   I'll never do nothing like that again.
SOONY.   My sister'll be here soon. I'll let her cuss you out.
MARY.   Your sister don't have to tell me to go. Won't you kiss me goodbye in decent friendship before I leave you?
SOONY.   Well — *(Mary kisses him and hugs his neck, touching as she does a leather thong hanging around it.)* Leave that alone!
MARY.   All right. *(She steps back.)* Goodbye, Soony.
SOONY.   Goodbye, Mary. *(Soony has another coughing fit.)*
MARY.   You want me to hold you?
SOONY.   No!
MARY.   How about some sassafras tea?
SOONY.   No!
MARY.   Whiskey then.
SOONY.   Git out!
MARY.   I'll put together my few things. *(Mary goes off the platform, but turns and waits, listening. Soony, alone, is frightened.)*
SOONY.   Jesus God. Oh!!! *(He coughs again, spitting into a handkerchief. He looks in it.)* Mary!! *(Mary steps up to the platform.)*
MARY.   Soony?
SOONY.   I'm bleeding in my lungs!
MARY.   Oh, Soony!
SOONY.   Get me something!
MARY.   You want the whiskey?
SOONY.   Yes!
MARY.   All right! *(She gets him whiskey in a cup and sets it on the table with Vangey's kerchief.)* And there's them cherry bark bitters you liked.
SOONY.   Let me have 'em.
MARY.   Here. *(She opens the kerchief, and the paper. Soony puts a little in his whiskey.)* Best take as much as you can.
SOONY.   All of it! *(Soony dumps the deadly powders into his whiskey, stirs it with a finger. He drinks.)*
MARY.   Is that better?
SOONY.   Some.
MARY.   You want me gone?
SOONY.   Not yet.

MARY.   I'll stay, then I'll go.
SOONY.   We'll see.
MARY.   Drink some more.
SOONY.   All right. *(He drinks all in his cup. Pause. He sighs.)* Them bitters feel good.
MARY.   They'll help you no end.
SOONY.   I forgive you, Mary.
MARY.   You do?
SOONY.   Hot boy. I'm old.
MARY.   Oh, Soony, hush.
SOONY.   Them Lovels did apologize.
MARY.   Yes, they did.
SOONY.   This is doing me good. Hold me tight.
MARY.   I will. *(Soony closes his eyes and breathes deeply, in relief. Enter Vangey and Nancy.)*
VANGEY.   See Nancy? There's your Daddy in your step-momma's arms. We don't have to get his sister after all. Go kiss him, too. *(Enter Logan and Ab. Nancy goes and kisses Soony. Vangey motions to Ab and Logan to follow her and goes to the porch.)* What a fine sight. The wife and the husband and the child.
AB.   Glory be to God! *(Vangey pulls a chair up to Soony, Mary and Nancy. Ab and Logan stand behind her. They all watch Soony sleep. They whisper.)*
VANGEY.   Did he drink the bitters?
MARY.   He did!
AB.   Hallelujah.
VANGEY.   Hallelujah.
MARY.   How long before he's better?
VANGEY.   Soon.
MARY.   How soon?
VANGEY.   After his nap.
AB.   He looks better right now.
VANGEY.   Say something.
AB.   My God, I will come to you in my distress. In my right hand is the sword I will lay down in your name —
VANGEY.   How's he breathing?
MARY.   Shallow but easy.
AB.   — and in my left hand is the plow I will use in peace.

Let his love dwell in my heart and I will care for none other's.
MARY.   Is that the Bible?
VANGEY.   Sort of.
AB.   And I will say, let the day perish when I was born before I harm one hair on the head of the least of these. Him who has ears to hear, let him hear. *(Soony jerks in Mary and Nancy's arms.)*
SOONY.   Oh! *(His eyes wide, Soony stares around him.)* You come back!
VANGEY.   We heard you calling out.
AB.   Wouldn't leave you to no harm, man.
SOONY.   Well. *(He closes his eyes.)* I thank ye. *(Long pause.)*
NANCY.   Is Daddy all right?
VANGEY.   He needs his sleep.
AB.   Breathing easy.
VANGEY.   See, Nancy?
NANCY.   I'm just scared is all. *(Nancy goes and embraces her father and her stepmother again. Soony stirs, sighs. Half conscious, he mumbles:)*
SOONY.   Oh! Put me to bed, Mary. *(Mary, with help, gets him up. Soony looks at Vangey, then at Ab. Then he holds out his arm for Nancy and they exit.)*
VANGEY.   There. *(Music. Change of light. Exeunt Ab and Vangey. Logan stays onstage, looking at the house. Music, time passing. Logan looks around, with even more satisfaction. Logan sits in Soony's chair, draws the quilt up comfortably around his knees and reads his "True Crime" book. Lights change. Enter Sawdust.)*
LOGAN.   What you doing, Sawdust?
SAWDUST.   Getting to that table. Thinking I got to re-bevil the legs.
LOGAN.   Come up on the porch. *(Sawdust does.)* Have a seat. *(Sawdust does.)* Me and Mary Sparks going to the county seat to marry next week. That bother you?
SAWDUST.   No, sir.
LOGAN.   She's a healthy woman. He was a sick man for a long time.
SAWDUST.   Not a word from me.
LOGAN.   I will run this farm. I ain't certain about your job.

SAWDUST.   I understand.

LOGAN.   We just don't know each other very well.

SAWDUST.   Whichever way, I wish you happiness.

LOGAN.   I don't mean who are you and where do you come from, I don't care about that. I just mean what are you? It's hard to see.

SAWDUST.   I'm just a fool, no two ways about that. Dumb as a yeller dog about most things. But I'm honest, I'll tell it to you, and I know farming up and down any slope in these mountains. But whatever you say, I'll do.

LOGAN.   There's just something slippery about you. What do you work here for, anyhow, all day and half the nights? You're so obliging, it's more than I can see the reason for.

SAWDUST.   This home, your home come next week, is a refuge. I been worse places, praise God. I feel safe here. I didn't used to be like this. Time was, I feared no man, no God and no thing. I'd take to drink and I'd drink. Drink my hat, drink my shirt, drink my shoes. That was me, scared of nobody, long as I had whiskey. I'd spit in the devil's face and tell *him* go to hell! But I met your daddy, went to his church and got his religion. I am a different man now, praise God. Thanks to good people like you and your fine upstanding daddy.

LOGAN.   My daddy does say you deserve consideration.

SAWDUST.   We have prayed mightily together.

LOGAN.   I'll keep you on.

SAWDUST.   Thank you, Logan.

LOGAN.   Sir.

SAWDUST.   Mr. Logan, sir. I thank you.

LOGAN.   Work on them barn walls first and then the table. And see to Nancy, you hear?

SAWDUST.   Yes, sir. *(Sawdust moves away, but stops and listens. Enter Nancy. She carries a cardboard box.)*

NANCY.   Hello, Logan.

LOGAN.   How you getting along?

NANCY.   I miss my daddy. But I know he suffered and is delivered now. I got Mary to take care of me. You, too, I hope.

LOGAN.   Of a sartin.

NANCY.   Next Friday?

LOGAN.   At the county seat. Will you come with us?
NANCY.   I'd kind of be your daughter.
LOGAN.   Kind of.
NANCY.   I'm content with it. Are you?
LOGAN.   Forever and ever.
NANCY.   Will you tell me about things in your books?
LOGAN.   I'll even read you some.
NANCY.   I'll hold you to it. And I'll come to your wedding.
(*Music. Change of light. Nancy goes to stand in a soft light. Logan stares at her. She takes off her overalls, stands naked, and then from the cardboard box, takes a flour sack dress and slowly puts it on, Logan watching. Lights change back. Music ends. Nancy sits with Logan again. Logan lays the quilt over both their knees.*)
LOGAN.   LYDIA SHERMAN, THE ARSENIC FIEND!
NANCY.   Lydia Sherman, the arsenic fiend!
LOGAN.   First husband, a carpenter.
NANCY.   First husband, a carpenter!
LOGAN.   Arsenic in the oatmeal.
NANCY.   Arsenic in the oatmeal!
LOGAN.   Second husband, a dentist.
NANCY.   A dentist!
LOGAN.   Arsenic in the baking soda!
NANCY.   In the baking soda!
LOGAN.   Third husband, a banker.
NANCY.   A banker!
LOGAN.   So she's rich, but she can't stop!
NANCY.   Can't stop!
LOGAN.   In his Brandy Slings!
NANCY.   In his Brandy Slings!
LOGAN.   And the banker dies!
NANCY.   The banker dies!
LOGAN.   Now she's rich! But!
NANCY.   But!
LOGAN.   The Banker's daughter. She gets all three bodies dug up. They find a truckload of arsenic in ever one, and Lydia Sherman confesses. This poem is her very own words. "I'll never know joy no more —"
NANCY.   "I'll never know joy no more —"

LOGAN.   "My life is as short as the rabbit —"
NANCY.   "My life is as short as the rabbit —"
LOGAN.   "I could not give it up —"
NANCY.   "I could not give it up —"
LOGAN.   "My good old arsenic habit!"
NANCY.   "My good old arsenic habit!" (*Nancy and Logan laugh. Logan exits. Nancy watches him, takes her box and goes into the house. Music. Change of light. Sawdust walks up onto the porch. He looks around a moment, then walks back off it and exits. Music ends. Enter Mary, grim. She puts the rocking chair to one side, a slat chair opposite it, and another slat chair at C. She sits in the rocker, rocks furiously and waits. Enter Vangey.*)
VANGEY.   Where is she?
MARY.   Coming.
VANGEY.   Where's Logan?
MARY.   Where else? Laying under a tree somewheres, reading true crime. (*Enter Nancy.*)
NANCY.   You wanted to see me?
MARY.   Have a seat. (*Nancy sits down with them.*)
NANCY.   I thank you kindly.
MARY.   All growed up about this, are you?
NANCY.   I understand it, if that's what you mean?
MARY.   Then what do you expect to be done about it?
NANCY.   Nothing you *can* do about it.
MARY.   Just let it happen?
NANCY.   This farm was my daddy's. It's half mine!
MARY.   Other wife, is it?
NANCY.   Why not?
MARY.   We can say it was Sawdust give you that baby and throw you both out on the road!
NANCY.   Who'd believe you?
MARY.   Who wouldn't?
VANGEY.   Maybe just a word here?
MARY.   From you? You said a potion could take care of her!
VANGEY.   Too late now.
NANCY.   I'd a never drank it noways. I want this baby!
VANGEY.   Does Logan know?
NANCY.   No.

MARY.   She wasn't telling *nobody* 'til it showed!
NANCY.   That's right!
MARY.   I could kill you dead.
VANGEY.   Now, Mary. You don't aim to wreck and ruin everything we built up here, just because your husband fouled the nest a little.
MARY.   A *little?*
NANCY.   He didn't fancy what he was getting from you, so leave me alone!
MARY.   On the road! I'll throw you out on the road! *(Enter Ab. He sits on the edge of the porch.)*
NANCY.   I couldn't help it! I didn't come after him —
VANGEY.   Just one word!
MARY.   Hell you didn't!
NANCY.   He come —
MARY.   Swishing your damn little —
VANGEY.   A word, I say —
NANCY.   After me!! You seen it! Did you throw him out of bed? No! He lies around reading books all day! He tells you woman this and woman that. My poor old daddy, you could get all around him, but Logan has you rag limp the minute you see him. Confess it!
VANGEY.   My son is a walking horn! You seen that from the beginning!
NANCY.   I seen it!
VANGEY.   Well, the bread's in the oven! What now?
NANCY.   I'll have our baby!
MARY.   And live here in scandal, with you lording it over me? I'll die first!
AB.   Look to the tender grapes and invite the bridegroom to the feast, for it is the happy family that will dwell in the house of the Lord. Amen!
VANGEY.   Amen! *(They stare at Ab.)*
NANCY.   Amen, what?
AB.   God is love.
VANGEY.   Amen!
NANCY.   WHAT? *(Pause.)*
AB.   We have some acquaintance with the Stoneman family.

MARY.   Stonemans?
NANCY.   Like in Bob Stoneman?
AB.   None other.
VANGEY.   Bob Stoneman allows that yes, his boy Fred is of a marrying age when and if.
AB.   When there's a bride and if there's a settlement.
MARY.   When did this happen?
AB.   When they left the Baptists.
VANGEY.   Course, you'll have to give the Stonemans a considerable something.
MARY.   How much?
VANGEY.   I say fifty acre. Twenty-five for them, twenty-five for us.
MARY.   Us?
VANGEY.   Out of two hundred? We are saving you, and your husband, and your farm, from a scandal make you wish you'd never been born! Why not us?
NANCY.   A Stoneman boy might marry me?
VANGEY.   That's the notion.
MARY.   Like that, better'n Logan?
NANCY.   I might.
MARY.   Thought so!
VANGEY.   Bob Stoneman's boy will do what he's told.
AB.   For twenty-five acre, they'll tell him.
NANCY.   I'll sorrow for my Logan.
MARY.   *Your* Logan?
VANGEY.   Let her finish!
NANCY.   But this is reasonable. I trust I will make Fred Stoneman a good wife. Yes, I'll have him.
VANGEY.   Good, that's that.
NANCY.   So it's settled.
MARY.   No, it's not! She's pregnant!
VANGEY.   Plainly is!
MARY.   Who'll take a wife with another man's baby in her?
AB.   How far gone?
NANCY.   'Bout three and a half.
AB.   Say she's living with her grandmother over the state line. Hint at it, but hold off the actual proposal for three. Dicker

and dispute it another two. That's eight and a half. Then the Stonemans won't fault a serious bride taking a devotional retreat, to prepare for holy matrimony.

VANGEY.   That'll do it. I'll midwife the birth, and nobody'll know a thing.

NANCY.   And I'll keep it?

VANGEY.   No, get found abandoned. County orphanage, honey. *(Nancy puts her chair back where it was. So do Mary and Vangey.)*

NANCY.   Babies die there.

VANGEY.   Not all of 'em.

NANCY.   I dread that place for a child of mine.

VANGEY.   Lady rich or slut poor? Take your choice.

NANCY.   I'm considering it.

VANGEY.   With a fine wedding and everthing. I'm being generous.

NANCY.   It had *better* be a fine wedding.

MARY.   What does that mean?

NANCY.   I know what you did to my daddy, with Vangey's deadly nightroot or something. *(Nancy faces them.)* One, two, maybe all three of you. So if I can't have Logan, you *best* get me Fred Stoneman, or somebody like him.

VANGEY.   Or what?

NANCY.   You know god damned well what. *(Enter Logan.)*

LOGAN.   Hey.

MARY.   Logan.

VANGEY.   Son. *(Exeunt Mary and Vangey.)*

AB.   Vengeance is mine, sayeth the Lord. Out of the whirlwind, I will come to you. *(Exit Ab. Music. Change of light. Logan stands onstage. Slow music. Time passes. Moonlight. Music dies away. Screams of Nancy in labor, with Mary and Vangey helping her. Logan paces the porch, agitated. Enter Sawdust.)*

SAWDUST.   How you doing?

LOGAN.   They told me I had to stay here on the porch. Ain't decent, a man this close to it. Is that whiskey?

SAWDUST.   Right here.

LOGAN.   I thought you didn't drink no more.

SAWDUST.   I brought it for you.

LOGAN.   Well, give it here. *(Sawdust gives Logan the jar, and Logan drinks. As he is drinking, Nancy is heard behind the porch, crying out, in labor.)*
NANCY.   *(Offstage.)* Ohhhh! Ohhh!
LOGAN.   Oh, Jesus!
SAWDUST.   There she goes.
LOGAN.   A man ought not to hear this!
NANCY.   *(Offstage.)* OHHHH!!!!!
LOGAN.   Oh, Jesus!
SAWDUST.   The time has come! *(Exit Sawdust.)*
LOGAN.   Sawdust? *(Logan drinks. Nancy's cries grow softer.)* Damn!!! *(Enter Ab, with a large shovel. He puts it at Logan's feet.)*
AB.   From the rib of Adam I say, take unto wife this woman Eve. Women are the will of God, son. We do the best we can. The Lord is my shepherd. I shall not want. I shall go to the mountains of Solomon. His eye is on the sparrow. Give me that. *(Ab drinks Logan's whiskey. Enter Mary.)*
MARY.   You fools stop drinking! The baby's born.
LOGAN.   Thank God.
MARY.   Did you give him the shovel?
AB.   Right yonder.
LOGAN.   I ain't studying no shovel. Baby's going to the orphanage.
MARY.   You'll take it there?
LOGAN.   No.
MARY.   Why not?
LOGAN.   Because I don't do such as that! I'm the man!
MARY.   The man, are you? All high and mighty with your big hard pecker, strutting about with the pride of it, throwing me down and having me like you please. Then sticking it to a girl, bringing her screaming to bastard childbirth? Man? YOU?
LOGAN.   Don't say no more!
MARY.   Dig the hole.
LOGAN.   Dig the what?
MARY.   Take the shovel and dig the hole.
AB.   I'll go back inside and help out.
LOGAN.   Daddy!

AB.   You take care of it! *(Exit Ab.)*
LOGAN.   This has got to be done some other way.
MARY.   How?
LOGAN.   Get it to the orphanage.
MARY.   Somebody will tell. Goodbye, Stoneman wedding.
(Vangey appears, quickly.)
VANGEY.   Get in here! *(Exit Vangey. Logan paces again.)*
MARY.   Do it, Logan!
LOGAN.   Not me!
MARY.   It's your baby!
LOGAN.   Did you kill Soony?
MARY.   Nobody killed nobody.
LOGAN.   Tell me the truth.
MARY.   If anybody did, your mother did.
LOGAN.   Oh, Jesus.
MARY.   She give powders to me. I give them to him. What difference does that make now?
LOGAN.   I'll not have it, woman!!
MARY.   Then what will you have, you stupid son of a bitch? *(Exit Mary. Logan sits, head in his hands. Enter Vangey and Ab.)*
VANGEY.   It's born. Did you do it?
LOGAN.   Do what?
VANGEY.   What your wife told you to!
LOGAN.   I didn't dig no hole, if that's what you mean.
VANGEY.   That's what I mean.
LOGAN.   It's a living soul!
VANGEY.   No, it ain't. Born dead.
LOGAN.   Born dead?
VANGEY.   You never heard it cry, did you?
LOGAN.   No.
VANGEY.   Tiny little thing. 'Bout three, four pound. *(Enter Mary. She carries the newborn baby, wrapped in rags, with a piece of old quilt hanging over it.)*
MARY.   Here it is.
LOGAN.   Was it a boy or a girl?
MARY.   Girl.
VANGEY.   Wrapped tight?
MARY.   In pack rags. *(Ab picks up the shovel.)*

LOGAN.   I ain't doing this!
MARY.   Yes, you are. *(Ab holds out the shovel.)*
AB.   Here.
LOGAN.   Stay away from me! *(Vangey takes the baby from Mary and shoves it into Logan's arms.)*
VANGEY.   Here!
LOGAN.   No!
VANGEY.   I'm your mother, son!
AB.   And your father!
MARY.   And your wife!
VANGEY.   Bury it!
MARY.   In the barn!
VANGEY.   Under the pens!
AB.   Where it smells.
VANGEY.   And the sow'll git to it.
LOGAN.   Was she baptized?
VANGEY.   Forget that! It's dead!
LOGAN.   She had a soul, didn't she?
VANGEY.   Ab!
AB.   I baptize this child in the name of Jesus! Amen!
MARY.   Now go on!
VANGEY.   Go!
AB.   Go!
LOGAN.   All right!! *(Logan starts off, baby in one arm, shovel under another. Suddenly, he throws down the shovel.)* Jesus God, she's moving! She's alive!
VANGEY.   So? *(Logan sets the baby down on the edge of the porch.)*
LOGAN.   You said she was dead!
VANGEY.   She will be!!
LOGAN.   What! *(Ab, Vangey and Mary, on the porch, approach the baby.)*
AB.   Kill her, god damn it!
LOGAN.   How?
MARY.   Any how! You're the man!
VANGEY.   Kill her!
MARY.   Dirt poor all our lives?
VANGEY.   You want that?
AB.   You want that?

MARY.   Don't be a fool!
VANGEY.   Son!
AB.   Logan!
MARY.   Now!!
LOGAN.   Ah!!!! *(Howling, Logan runs back to the shovel, picks it up, runs back to the porch, brings the hilt of the shovel smashing down on the baby three savage times. Then he throws the shovel down. A long, deadly pause.)*
VANGEY.   Good, Logan.
AB.   All right, boy.
MARY.   Now you can bury it.
LOGAN.   I heard her bones crack. I hear them now! *(Vangey, Mary and Ab move quickly, Ab to Logan, Vangey to the baby, Mary to the shovel. Mary gives Logan the shovel, Vangey gives him the baby, Ab pushes him off.)*
VANGEY.   You can't hear nothing. You smashed her head in.
MARY.   Dig. *(The stage is quickly cleared. Wind, and cold light. The stage is empty for a moment. Enter Nancy, wrapped in the quilt, leaning on Mary. Vangey settles her in Soony's chair, under the quilt, while Mary hands her a mug of tea. Nancy sits in the rocking chair and sips the tea. Vangey and Mary stand by her. Enter Logan, slowly.)*
VANGEY.   Come on, son.
MARY.   She's all right.
VANGEY.   She didn't break.
MARY.   Come see.
NANCY.   You don't have to stare at me. I'm alive.
MARY.   You two have a nice talk. *(Mary and Vangey step back.)*
LOGAN.   You still hurting?
NANCY.   What from?
LOGAN.   The baby.
NANCY.   I see no baby here.
LOGAN.   What?
NANCY.   I took sick with a fever. I lost my bearings.
LOGAN.   We had a baby, Nancy.
NANCY.   You had it. I didn't.
LOGAN.   How can you say that?
NANCY.   Just open my mouth and say it. You're a fool,

Logan. You read them silly books and think you know all about it and you don't.

LOGAN.   You have every right to be fired up at me.

NANCY.   I ain't fired up, I'm cold as a creek. When I marry Fred Stoneman, I will treat you with the disdain you deserve. *(Nancy finishes the tea. To Vangey and Mary, calmly.)* That was good. *(She hands the mug to Vangey.)* Take me back to bed. *(Mary and Vangey come to her, help her up, wrap the quilt around her.)*

MARY.   We can tell the Stoneman family?

NANCY.   Why not?

VANGEY.   Ab can do it?

NANCY.   I said, why not?

MARY.   You were sick but now you're well?

NANCY.   How many times do I have to say yes?

VANGEY.   We can bring them here, and all get together? Be sure, now!

NANCY.   I won't fall down, if that's what you mean.

VANGEY.   That's what I mean.

MARY.   Say tomorrow night. Vangey?

VANGEY.   Nancy?

NANCY.   Tomorrow night. I'll be ready.

VANGEY.   Come on, honey. We'll take care of you. *(Nancy almost falls, then shakes them off.)*

NANCY.   I can walk by myself! *(Nancy walks into the house, with Mary and Vangey. Logan starts to follow them. The three women turn and stare at him. He steps back. Music. Lights and shadows. Time passes. Logan paces on the porch. He takes from his pocket a mason jar with a clear liquid in it. He drinks and paces. He drinks and paces. Enter Sawdust.)*

SAWDUST.   Hidy.

LOGAN.   Sawdust?

SAWDUST.   Logan.

LOGAN.   Where you been? *(Sawdust walks up onto the porch, looking around. He carries a thick walking stick. He is no longer so agreeable.)*

SAWDUST.   Up one side the mountain, down the other. What you drinking?

LOGAN.   Paint thinner.
SAWDUST.   I knowed a man went blind drinking that.
LOGAN.   They won't give me no likker. Say I got to be sober today. Have some?
SAWDUST.   No. *(Logan drinks.)* Killed it, did ye? *(Logan drinks.)* Where'd ye put it? *(Logan drinks.)* In the barn?
AB. *(Offstage.)* Logan! *(Sawdust moves back. Enter Ab.)* The Stoneman family will be here any minute. *(Ab throws a black coat on the chair.)* Get in this and get ready! *(Exit Ab.)*
SAWDUST.   Stoneman family? At's what I heard. Then you best make it right.
LOGAN.   How?
SAWDUST.   Find peace.
LOGAN.   HOW?
SAWDUST.   You know how. *(Enter Mary.)*
MARY.   Logan! *(Sees Sawdust.)* Oh, my God!
SAWDUST.   Hidy.
MARY.   What's he doing here?
SAWDUST.   I come to this big meeting between the Stonemans and the Lovels and the Sparks.
MARY.   You ain't welcome! Get him out of here! *(Sawdust smiles and sits on the porch steps.)*
SAWDUST.   I know she had a baby.
NANCY.   Get him gone!
LOGAN.   Do it yourself. *(Logan drinks. Enter Vangey and Ab.)*
AB.   Sawdust?
SAWDUST.   Who ain't welcome here no more. But who told Vangey Lovel that Soony Sparks was sick and his wife after her boy! Who for Ab Lovel brought the Stoneman family in to Jesus! And now, who is here to help everbody find peace and you know what that is. *(Deadly pause.)* He could confess it.
MARY.   Oh, God.
SAWDUST.   At this meeting. Or I can do it for him.
VANGEY.   Don't do that. *(To Mary.)* Come on. *(They exit. Ab stares at Sawdust, takes a threatening step toward him. Sawdust takes from its sheath a dangerous looking knife and taps it against his walking stick. Ab steps back.)*
AB.   What you been saying to my son?

SAWDUST.   Same as you said to me. Make it right.
AB.   We are doing that.
SAWDUST.   I'm waiting.
AB.   What else you doing?
SAWDUST.   Being what you said I'd be, if I listened to you.
Happy.
AB.   With your sinful wife.
SAWDUST.   I don't have no wife. I never did. *(Enter Mary
and Vangey. Vangey slaps a brown envelope into Sawdust's hand,
backs away from him.)*
VANGEY.   You'll never see that much money in one place
in your whole life. *(Sawdust looks at the money quickly.)*
SAWDUST.   About five hundred dollar? That's not right.
VANGEY.   What *is?*
SAWDUST.   He kept his money off a string around his throat.
Ten times this.
AB.   You damned drunk!
SAWDUST.   EVER *SEE* ME DRUNK? I can tell the Stonemans
dig up the barn. I know there was five thousand dollar.
VANGEY.   Get it. *(Mary starts off.)*
SAWDUST.   No. *(To Ab.)* You get it.
AB.   I don't know where it is.
VANGEY.   Go with her. *(Exit Mary and Ab. Sawdust sticks his
knife into the porch, where it stands by him. Vangey sits on the porch
steps next to the knife and Sawdust. She almost smiles with him.)*
We miscalculated you.
SAWDUST.   I reckon.
VANGEY.   Like a tree in the mist. First you see it, then you
don't, then you do again.
SAWDUST.   I get by.
VANGEY.   How do you get by? Tell a body.
SAWDUST.   I look for the right church.
VANGEY.   You have just fooled with us.
SAWDUST.   And enjoyed it. *(Vangey slowly reaches toward
Sawdust's knife. Sawdust grips his walking stick. Vangey reverses the
knife, hands it back to Sawdust, handle toward him.)*
VANGEY.   So. *(Enter Ab and Mary, who carries a leather bag.)*
MARY.   Here.

SAWDUST.   Let him. *(Mary hands the leather bag to Ab, who hands it to Sawdust. He opens it, looks, closes it.)* I thank you. So long, folks. *(Sawdust gets up, starts off, stops.)* A fool can always find a bigger fool to worship God with him. Bye, Logan. *(Exit Sawdust. Pause. They all stay right where they are.)*

AB.   This could have been worse.

VANGEY.   How much did we save?

MARY.   A thousand.

VANGEY.   Logan?

AB.   Are you listening to us?

MARY.   They're coming, Logan!

AB.   The whole Stoneman family!

MARY.   What's the matter with you?

VANGEY.   When it was time to take, you took. Now it is time to give.

LOGAN.   In one minute.

VANGEY.   One minute. *(Vangey nods to the others. They exit with her. Logan drinks again, shivers, sits on the edge of the porch, drinks and stares bleakly ahead of him.)*

LOGAN.   *(To himself.)* Judge Beal. Fatty Harper. Lumberjack Jake. Lydia Sherman. Logan Lovel. *(Change of light. Wind rises. Against it, a clear voice of a young girl is heard, singing in the wind.)*

VOICE IN THE WIND.   *(Singing.)*
> BY THY LAST SILENCE
> IN THE JUDGMENT HALL,
> BY LONG FOREKNOWLEDGE
> OF THE DEADLY TREE.
> BY DARKNESS, BY THE WORMWOOD
> AND THE GALL,
> I PRAY THOU VISIT ME.*

(Wind, loud, then fades. Light changes back. Enter Jennie.)

JENNIE.   Logan?

LOGAN.   Huh.

JENNIE.   Logan, it's me.

* See Special Note on Songs and Recordings on copyright page.

LOGAN.   Jennie?
JENNIE.   I come by. My husband brought me.
LOGAN.   Here?
JENNIE.   He's in the wagon yonder. He wanted me to come see you.
LOGAN.   Anson Tate?
JENNIE.   He's good, Logan. Hard, but fair. I told him about us, and he brought me here, to say something to you.
LOGAN.   Say what?
JENNIE.   I'm with his child.
LOGAN.   Is that so?
JENNIE.   My husband says he wants you to know he comprehends we cared for each other, and he honors that. You will always be welcome in our home.
LOGAN.   He said that?
JENNIE.   And means it.
LOGAN.   Tell him I am much obliged.
JENNIE.   I will. And — I want to ask you something.
LOGAN.   Ask.
JENNIE.   "If a better one you'll forget, if a worse one you'll remember." Which did you do?
LOGAN.   I did first one, then the other.
JENNIE.   Both. I had to ask.
LOGAN.   Now let me ask you.
JENNIE.   Anything.
LOGAN.   Would I have made a good husband, a good father?
JENNIE.   You'd have learned.
LOGAN.   You believe that?
JENNIE.   I do.
LOGAN.   But what do you think of me now?
JENNIE.   I'm no judge.
LOGAN.   Be mine.
JENNIE.   I've seen worse.
LOGAN.   You just think you have.
JENNIE.   That may be. But love is blind.
LOGAN.   Can I touch the baby?
JENNIE.   Why?
LOGAN.   Please.

JENNIE.   Here. (*Jennie lifts her blouse. Logan very gently kneels, rests both hands and then his cheek on her bare stomach. Jennie smiles and touches his head, lightly. For a moment, they look like a young man and wife, waiting for a baby. Then Logan gets up, steps back sternly.*)
LOGAN.   Don't let it cry too much.
JENNIE.   I won't.
LOGAN.   Don't spoil it neither.
JENNIE.   I won't.
LOGAN.   Anson Tate will make it a good daddy.
JENNIE.   I trust he will.
LOGAN.   He'll be wanting you now.
JENNIE.   Yes.
LOGAN.   Bye.
JENNIE.   Bye. (*Exit Jennie. Logan looks at his whiskey, then screws the top back on the jar. Enter first Mary, then Ab, then Vangey. They stare at Logan in deadly silence. A long pause.*)
MARY.   What are you going to do?
LOGAN.   What I ought to do.
MARY.   Confess, Logan?
LOGAN.   I might!
MARY.   Oh, God.
AB.   Tell what you done?
LOGAN.   And hang, like a man, yes!
MARY.   I'd hang with you!
AB.   Your mother, too?
MARY.   That what you want?
LOGAN.   Maybe it is! (*Vangey goes to Logan, with his coat.*)
VANGEY.   Then you should put on your coat like a man. (*Logan puts his arms through the sleeves.*) There. Look your best when you face it. What you'll have to do. (*Vangey points ahead of them.*) Yonder's a judge. Tell him who done what.
LOGAN.   My wife and my mother —
VANGEY.   My wife and my mother —
LOGAN.   Poisoned Soony Sparks.
VANGEY.   Poisoned Soony Sparks. Then I, Logan Lovel —
LOGAN.   Then I, Logan Lovel, got his daughter with a baby girl.

VANGEY.   Then I, Logan Lovel —
LOGAN.   Then I, Logan Lovel, killed her the night she was
           born.
         Hang me in darkness,
         By the light of the moon,
         To my child let me say
         I will be with you soon.
VANGEY.   And you will. That is a fine sentiment. That is
manly. But she can't hear you now, so does it matter when?
You, your mother, your father and your wife, like those who
done the same and worse, will pass away and be with her, too,
but not before our time, which will arrive. *(Vangey takes Logan
by the arm, gently.)* Possess yourself, Logan. Stand up with your
family. *(Logan shakes her off and stands apart. Vangey looks out
from the porch.)* Here come the Stonemans. *(Enter Nancy from
the house, brightly dressed, looking healthy. She takes her place with
the others. Logan stares at them a moment. Then Logan takes his
place with his family. Ab, Vangey, Nancy, Logan and Mary, their
faces without expression, hold up their hands in a wave to the ap-
proaching Stonemans. They freeze. Cheerful mountain music. Lights
fade on them, frozen as they wave.)*

PROPERTY LIST

Book, *True Crimes* (LOGAN)
Old quilt (LOGAN, JENNIE, MARY, VANGEY AB)
Colorful quilt (SOONY)
Chest with bottle and whiskey glasses (SOONY)
Bowl of spoon bread (MARY)
Whimmey-diddle toy (NANCY)
Tray with mugs and mason jar glasses (NANCY)
Folded kerchief (VANGEY) with
      folded papers inside holding ground herbs
Government pamphlet (LOGAN)
Lock (SAWDUST)
Leather thong (SOONY)
Handkerchief (SOONY)
Cardboard box (NANCY) with
  flour-sack dress
Jar of whiskey (SAWDUST)
Large shovel (AB)
Figure size of baby, weighted to 3 pounds and wrapped in
      old cloth and piece of quilt (MARY)
Mug of tea (MARY)
Mason jar with clear liquid (LOGAN)
Walking stick (SAWDUST)
Large knife, with sheath (SAWDUST)
Leather bag (MARY)

SOUND EFFECTS

47

Wind

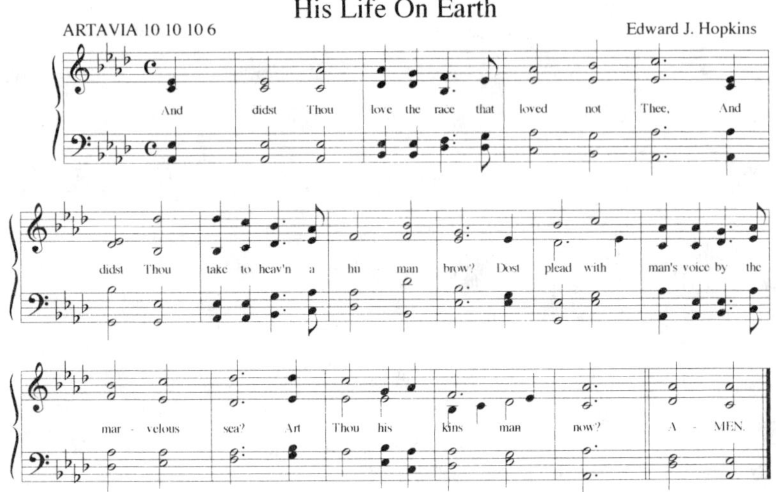

His Life On Earth

ARTAVIA 10 10 10 6

Edward J. Hopkins

(2)   By that one likeness which is ours and Thine,
       By that one nature which doth hold us kin,
By that high heaven where, sinless, Thou dost shine,
       To draw us sinners in;

(3)   By Thy last silence in the judgment-hall,
       By long foreknowledge of the deadly tree,
By darkness, by the wormwood and the gall,
       I pray Thee visit me.

(4)   Come, lest this heart should, cold and cast away,
       Die ere the guest adored she entertain;
Lest eyes which never saw Thine earthly day
       Should miss Thy heavenly reign.

- Jean Ingelow

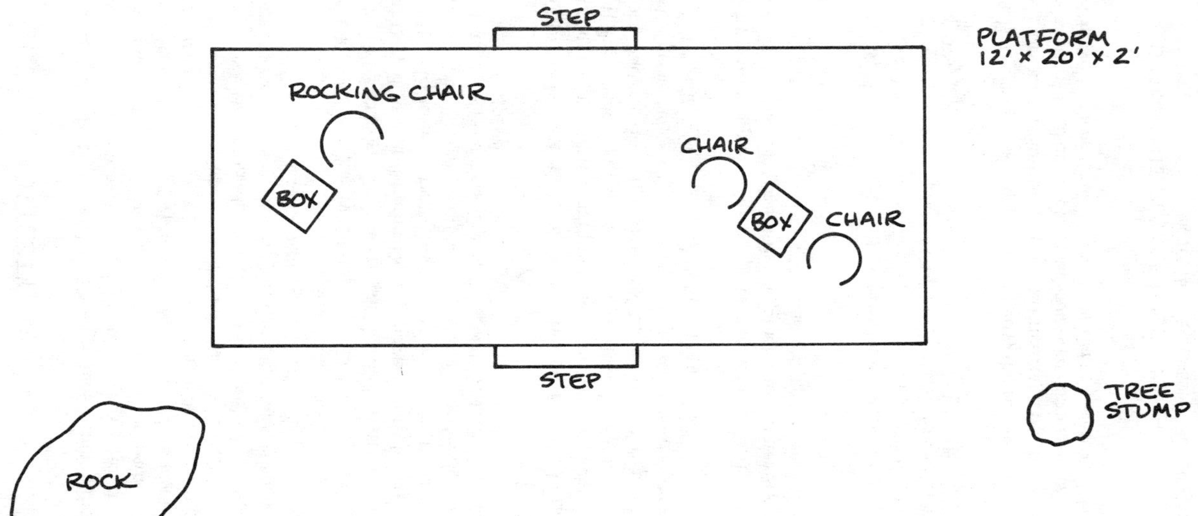

SCENE DESIGN

"TRUE CRIMES"

(DESIGNED BY E. DAVID COSIER FOR THEATER FOR THE NEW CITY)

TODAY'S HOTTEST NEW PLAYS

❑ **THREE VIEWINGS by Jeffrey Hatcher.** Three comic-dramatic monologues, set in a midwestern funeral parlor, interweave as they explore the ways we grieve, remember, and move on. *"Finally, what we have been waiting for: a new, true, idiosyncratic voice in the theater. And don't tell me you hate monologues; you can't hate them more than I do. But these are much more: windows into the deep of each speaker's fascinating, paradoxical, unique soul, and windows out into a gallery of surrounding people, into hilarious and horrific coincidences and conjunctions, into the whole dirty but irresistible business of living in this damnable but spellbinding place we presume to call the world." - New York Magazine.* [1M, 2W]

❑ **HAVING OUR SAY by Emily Mann.** The Delany Sisters' Bestselling Memoir is now one of Broadway's Best-Loved Plays! Having lived over one hundred years apiece, Bessie and Sadie Delany have plenty to say, and their story is not simply African-American history or women's history...it is our history as a nation. *"The most provocative and entertaining family play to reach Broadway in a long time." - New York Times. "Fascinating, marvelous, moving and forceful." - Associated Press.* [2W]

❑ **THE YOUNG MAN FROM ATLANTA Winner of the 1995 Pulitzer Prize. by Horton Foote.** An older couple attempts to recover from the suicide death of their only son, but the menacing truth of why he died, and what a certain Young Man from Atlanta had to do with it, keeps them from the peace they so desperately need. *"Foote ladles on character and period nuances with a density unparalleled in any living playwright." - NY Newsday.* [5M, 4W]

❑ **SIMPATICO by Sam Shepard.** Years ago, two men organized a horse racing scam. Now, years later, the plot backfires against the ringleader when his partner decides to come out of hiding. *"Mr. Shepard writing at his distinctive, savage best." - New York Times.* [3M, 3W]

❑ **MOONLIGHT by Harold Pinter.** The love-hate relationship between a dying man and his family is the subject of Harold Pinter's first full-length play since *Betrayal*. *"Pinter works the language as a master pianist works the keyboard." - New York Post.* [4M, 2W, 1G]

❑ **SYLVIA by A.R. Gurney.** This romantic comedy, the funniest to come along in years, tells the story of a twenty-two year old marriage on the rocks, and of Sylvia, the dog who turns it all around. *"A delicious and dizzy new comedy." - New York Times. "FETCHING! I hope it runs longer than Cats!" - New York Daily News.* [2M, 2W]

DRAMATISTS PLAY SERVICE, INC.
440 Park Avenue South, New York, New York 10016 212-683-8960 Fax 212-213-1539